Lindsey,
from your friend
Bill White

Wade H. Fee
July 11, 2011

Jornanda del Muerto, (journey of the dead man)

TALES
OF THE
CABALLOS
BY WILLIAM H. WHITE

Published by
William H. White

Printed by
Stanton Press
Saint Paul, Minnesota

November 2003
First Edition
ISBN 978-0-9800057-0-7

Dedication Page

This book is dedicated to all treasure hunters. May you be successful at whatever endeavor you choose. Remember, it is in the hunt that we gain the most satisfation.

William H. White

TALES OF THE CABALLOS

TABLE OF CONTENTS

Forward

To try to cover a subject as rich and as vast as the Caballos Mountains became more of a challenge as the book progressed. There are so many stories and so many people who richly deserve to be mentioned in this writing. I have tried to capture the essence of the time and place when the events took place to give the reader a better understanding of what it was like then as well as what it is like now. I regret that I could not include all of the stories surrounding this mountain.

I have purposefully not included some of the people who rightly deserve to be part of this story but because of their continuing commitment to the Caballos Mountains, I felt that it would be a major disservice to them to draw undue attention upon their activities at this writing. I apologize to anyone who feels slighted by this. In my opinion, it would be far better to feel slighted than to feel harassed by future treasure hunters who will be reading this book.

There are so many stories and people of whom I have never met who no doubt have a tale to tell that could only enrich this magnificent mountain lore. To them I apologize also, and say that it was only lack of knowledge on my part for not including them in this book in the first place.

I would especially like to thank James Neidig, Ron Strobel, John Vance, Don Snodgrass, Jerry Cheatum and Lewis Jameson for their invaluable insights and stories. Without these people this book would not have been possible. Thank you all for your generous help and support.

INTRODUCTION

DON FINGADO

No modern day history of the Caballos Mountains would be complete without mention of Don Fingado. Don spent most of his adult life in the steep canyons and rock faces of this mountain in search of that elusive dream, treasure. It is with some sadness that I am to report that Don Fingado was never successful with this endeavor.

Don Fingado was a graduate Mining Engineer and knew more about the geology of this mountain than anyone I have ever met. Don tried so hard for so many years and never succeeded but he came away from the mountain with a greater treasure by far. Don Fingado knew that the search is the real treasure and the Caballos Mountains always gives back a gift equal to or exceeding one's effort when one ventures there.

At this writing Don Fingado has died of bone cancer. His widow still lives in Truth or Consequences, New Mexico in a modest trailer on the banks of the Rio Grande River.

Don Fingado was always unfailingly polite to those who visited him but on some days he had such little energy he could barely function. In his prime, he was a man among men. There was never a person who could keep up with Don Fingado on the mountain. Don could run where most of us could scarcely crawl.

When Don was searching an area on the Caballos Mountains known as "dark Canyon", he built a modest cabin at the upper rim. Don had a trail from the cabin down to where he was digging that a Mountain Goat would have trouble with. Don walked this trail twice a day when he toiled there. The cabin is still on the rim south of the Taggert Claims. It is so remote that vandals haven't done much damage to it, mainly because they haven't found it to vandalize yet. Don Fingado's name is on the cabin so if you should come across it there will be no doubt in your mind that this is Don's abandoned cabin.

It is reported that in "dark Canyon" Don Fingado tunneled into the mountain for over fifty feet using only hand steel and explosives. This is a feat unknown today but common in the thirties and forties. Don Fingado was truly a man from the past.

Now that Don is gone, those of us who knew him still miss him. It is truly the end of an era now. One of the mountain Icons has moved on to a better place. This book is dedicated to the memory of Don Fingado. There will never be another one like you Don. Never.

Author's Note
In part one of this book I have focused on stories that reflect the Caballos Mountains with the onset of the European intrusion into the North American Continent. First came the Spaniards then the Jesuits to the Rio Grande valley and lands beyond to change forever the history and culture of this region. I am not sympathetic to any one historical group however I greatly admire great deeds such as those of the Spanish Conquistadors and the equally great deeds of the Apache Indians who opposed them.

PART ONE

CHAPTER ONE

THE CABALLOS MOUNTAINS

The Caballos Mountains stretch from north to south along the Rio Grande River for roughly twenty three miles beginning at the Elephant Butte Lake dam and ending somewhere close to Garfield, New Mexico to the south.

The western side of these mountains feature vertical limestone cliffs setting atop a black band of pre-Cambrian rock. (Before life on earth) What was once the Rio Grande river is now a lake called appropriately the "Caballo Reservoir", a shallow stretch of water about fifteen miles long.

To the east there are more trees and brush while the mountain gently rises to match the rim of the mountain. The tallest point is around eight thousand feet. When viewing the mountain from either the north or the south it takes on the appearance of an equilateral triangle. My first impression of this mountain was nothing special. I was to learn later just how wrong first impressions could be.

The Caballos Mountains were mined by the Aztec's for gold and used as a burial site for their people. The Aztecs were not the first ones to visit the mountain but for the sake not being too controversial in this writing, I am beginning this history with the Aztecs. We know the Aztecs were here because they left evidence on the Caballos Mountain as well as other mountain ranges in the surrounding area.

Next was the conquering Spaniards in search of the seven cities of Cibola. The Spaniards had gained access to the mountain and both mined and stored gold in and around the mountain. Groups of Spaniards remained at the mountain continuously until the 1680 Pueblo Revolt. Their signs are still visible to those who wander there although most have been either destroyed or hidden by the treasure hunters of the last century. Next came the Jesuits who eventually established nine missions on the Caballos Mountains. They were there until the 1680 Pueblo revolt and the story is best told in the Padre LaRue story.

Finally the Apache Indians played a major role in shaping the history of the Caballos Mountains. To the east of this mountain stretches a level plain that stretches for perhaps 100 miles with a Spanish road in the center called the Camino Real. This road can be seen to this day by air. It was the main traveling route taken by the Spanish going to and from Santa Fe and Mexico City. The Spanish gave this route a name, Jorinado Del Muerto, a name that this plain is still known by to this day. It translates to "Journey of the dead man" and for good reason. The Spaniards could carry only three days of water for themselves and their animals. Sometimes the water holes were dry and they had to push on to the next location in the hope that water would be found there. Then there were flash floods that would turn the road into an impassable quagmire, and finally, the Apache Indians who waged a 450-year war against the intruders from Europe. This was the chosen battleground for the Apache. This was not the ancestral tribal home of these Indians so the need to defend the land was not there. The Apaches could attack at a time and place of their own choosing and quickly leave the Jorinado Del Muerto when the raid was finished.

The Spanish responded in kind to the ferocity of the Apache. There was a bounty placed on the head of any Apache and it was paid unhesitatingly by the Spanish and later the Mexican government as well. The Apache was given no quarter and none were asked for. During this period The Apache were more than a match for their adversary. It wasn't until the coming of the American army that spelled doom for this mighty warrior race. They were met with an organized and relentless enemy that drove the Apaches into hiding and eventually destroyed their independence.

Of these three main groups of people, the Spanish were the first to mine and refine gold at the Caballos Mountains. It could be said that most but not all of the treasure left by this group is generally found at lower elevations. This same basic rule could apply to the second group, the Jesuits.

The Apache on the other hand generally stored their booty on the higher elevations of the Caballos. They looked for caves and natural outcroppings that were more common in the limestone. The Apache did not want gold and they felt it was wrong for the Spanish to mine it so when some gold was captured it was always given back to the earth. The Apache never intended to come back and retrieve the gold stored by them on the mountain.

This is the Caballos Mountains today. It is loaded with treasure sites from end to end and top to bottom. Those who have come before and been successful on this mountain have just scratched the surface. It is out there to this day waiting for the right person to come along and claim it.

CHAPTER TWO

THE SPANIARDS

No story of the Caballos Mountains would be complete without a thumb-nail sketch of the Spanish as it relates to the mountain. Most of the other stories of this book would not be true if not for the single minded quest of those amazing Europeans

The Spanish came to the new world with a single goal and while a few stayed and settled in the new land, most ultimately returned to Spain or simply died here. Four of ten Spaniards never survived the hostile environment with every hand turned against them in the new world. Those who survived went back to Spain in triumph with great wealth and honor.

The Spanish came for gold and they found much gold in the Caballos Mountains. Most of the gold bars still remaining in the mountain were placed there by the Spanish. Of course the Jesuits played a significant role, as did the Apaches by simply placing the bars back into the mountain when taken. By far, the most concentrations of gold bars were made by the Spanish.

In many respects the Spaniards have been given a bum-rap by the history books. They are usually seen as slavers and oppressors but that behavior was the exception to the rule. Most Spaniards learned soon enough that a little silver was usually enough to ensure a hardworking group of natives willing to work for them. This was always the preferred way to complete the mining activities.

Another problem facing the Spanish was that every felon and rapist in Spain who wanted to avoid justice could simply sign-on for the new world and disappear for twenty years or so.

16

There was an overabundance of unsavory people within the ranks of the Spanish in the new world and little restraint was used to prevent their misdeeds. This is more than likely the reason they were hated so much.

For the most part the Spaniards stayed to themselves and worked the mines. They arrived with all the skills of European civilization such as metallurgy, carpentry, millwright, black-smith, and etc., etc. Each expedition was independent and could live off the land while going about their business, and they were formidable fighters. A Spaniard in full Armor on horseback was a very difficult opponent to the scantily clad natives.

There remain a significant number of Spanish roads on the Caballos Mountains to this day. The amazing thing is that some of the roads are three hundred years old or older and can still be used to this date.

The main difference between the Spanish and the Europeans who settled North America is that the Spanish never wanted to stay. They only wanted the gold. I believe that this is the ultimate reason of why they were defeated and forcibly removed from the new world.

PART ONE

CHAPTER THREE

PADRE LARUE

Padre LaRue was a Jesuit Monk who arrived in Mexico City with his group of fellow French Jesuits around the early 1600's. Because his group's primary language was not Spanish, they were treated poorly by the authorities of the Catholic Church then stationed in Mexico City. Padre LaRue and his group were eventually relegated to an insignificant parish someplace in what is now the state of Chihuahua, Mexico. It was in this parish where the majority of the native population were treated little better than chattels by the Spanish, that LaRue began what was to be his life's work.

The records are sketchy as to why Padre LaRue migrated almost four hundred miles to the north with his parishioners but it is well known that this is what took place.

Padre LaRue first located in what is now known as the Organ Mountains. A rather spectacular pile of rocks located just to the west of what is now Las Cruces, New Mexico. His foundations can be seen in the ruins of a hotel that flourished there in the early 1900's. The place is now called Dripping Springs and is administered by the Bureau of Land Management. The hike into this place is well worth the effort. The ruins are well hidden to the west of the spring in the heart of the canyon while surrounded by trees and brush.

It is not known at this writing just how long Padre LaRue and his followers stayed at this location but the Jesuit story as it relates to the Caballos Mountains is the meat of this writing. The Caballos Mountains lie almost due north the Organ Mountains, about sixty-five miles as the crow flies.

The Jesuits established nine missions in and around the

Caballos Mountains and soon were flourishing with the help of their original parishioners as well as the help of the friendly Apache Indians who had villages near there on the Rio Grande River. These missions were established with two criteria in mind. First there had to be year around water available and secondly there had to be gold that could be mined close by. The Jesuits believed that they answered to no one but the Pope in Rome and their mission here in the new world was to create new riches for the church. This policy proved to be their undoing in later years.

During this era, the Jesuits were left to themselves by the Spanish authorities as they went about their business of mining and stockpiling gold. Secondarily, the Jesuits were dedicated to saving the soles of the poor ignorant Native Americans who happened to live close by. I am certain that the Jesuits gained access to the mountain during their tenure there. Eye witnesses have reported seeing hastily stacked coffins and church records in the bowels of the mountain.

Padre LaRue eventually died and was buried by the Apache Indians in the mountain. He was sitting at his desk with his papers around him when seen by both Buster Ward and Willie Doughit. These two simply went about removing gold bars and had little use with disturbing the dead. Doc. Noss on the other hand did not share this fear of disturbing the spirits. It was from under the hand of Padre LaRue that Doc. Noss located the maps and descriptions that eventually took him to Victorio Peak on what is now the White Sands Missile Range. I am fairly certain that Padre LaRue is buried on the Caballos Mountains and much of what we know of him today we owe to Doc Noss.

It is not known how much gold was hoarded by the Jesuits but it would be safe to say that it was substantial. The Jesuits were on the Caballos Mountains about sixty years until events beyond their control caused them to abandon these mountains forever. Given the human resources and the time the Jesuits had to mine and hoard gold, the actual numbers would be staggering. No one can begin to estimate the value of the Gold mined and stock piled during the era. It was well known that few of these

Jesuit gold bars actually reached Europe because of the Jesuits refusal to pay the kings taxes on gold produced in the new world.

The real tragedy struck around 1680 during the depths of the worst drought in the history of New Mexico. It was this drought that triggered what was to become known as the 1680 Pueblo Revolt. The drought was so severe that the Rio Grande River went dry, the Game left the area and the crops failed. The Indians blamed the Spanish. It was certainly their fault that the Gods were angry and punishing the Indians with this drought. The Indians saw no difference between the Spanish and the Jesuits. All must be driven off or killed to end this tragedy.

The Jesuits hastily closed up the mines they were working, buried the church records and artifacts, and ran for their lives. The Spanish were driven back to El Paso Del Norte to the south and did not return for thirty years. The Jesuits never returned to the Caballos Mountains. They had fallen into disfavor by the Spanish Crown and many went back to Spain in chains.

The Jesuits were eventually replaced by the Franciscans who were more than willing to pay taxes. The old missions on the Caballos Mountains were never re-opened. The mines worked by the Jesuits were hidden by the Indians during the revolt and most were forgotten, never to be re-opened again. The Jesuits were gone forever from this part of New Mexico but they left their mark on the mountain. There is no doubt that these enterprising Europeans left hoard after hoard of gold bars most of which is waiting to this day for some lucky treasure hunter to stumble onto.

CHAPTER FOUR

PEDRO NAVARREZ

Pedro Navarrez was an outlaw who flourished in the vicinity of the Caballos Mountains in the mid 1600's. He was half Apache and half Spanish and was at home in either culture. He could use a block and tackle or a bow and arrow with equal effectiveness. Pedro decided upon a life of crime at an early age when he single-handedly stole six horses from a rival Indian tribe. Pedro was only twelve years old at the time. He brought the horses into the Apache camp where he was heralded a hero by his Indian family. Stealing from others outside the tribe was not considered a crime by the Apaches but rather an honorable endeavor.

Pedro soon focused upon the most hated group of the Apaches enemies, the Spaniards. The Spaniard's comings and goings along the Camino Real in the Jouranado Del Muerto provided easy prey for this ambitious young man. Pedro soon gathered a group of Indians around him to assist in his raids. The number of his band grew to an incredible 600 braves at the time of his defeat and capture.

Although he was quite young and ambitious his rein of terror existed for only twelve years. During this time Pedro accumulated a vast amount of loot taken from his Spanish adversaries. Unlike the Spanish, Pedro preferred silver to gold. Silver could be traded for gunpowder or knives at the Spanish trading posts without raising eyebrows. Gold on the other hand could not be traded openly without arousing suspicion.

Pedro Navarrez had been raiding and pillaging virtually unchecked until one of his acts infuriated the Spanish. Pedro and his band attacked and sacked one of the Jesuit missions on the western slope of the Caballos Mountains, killing the inhabitants and taking the church treasure. The response by the Spanish was quick and overwhelming to this outlaw band.

A well disciplined detachment of Spanish solders appeared almost immediately with full body armor and field cannon. Pedro and his band were totally unprepared for this and attempted to flee. Pedro quickly headed for a pass in the southern reaches of the Caballos Mountains that was to eventually be called "Apache Gap" in later years. His plan was to disburse into the Jouranado Del Muerto. The Spanish were waiting for him and he never made it. It was here that Pedro Navarrez was captured with all of his men after a brisk two-day battle. The Spanish quickly put the surviving members of his gang to death while Pedro Navarrez was taken to Mexico City to stand trial.

Pedro Navarrez was sentenced to death but he converted to Christianity before his execution. In his quest for divine forgiveness he described the location of his main treasure stash and it is this description that has tantalized treasure hunters to this day.

"Where three springs meet, look for a rock that is not of the area. Look for a gray flat stone with a crude cross or X on it. Under this stone you will find etc" This is not an exact translation but the reader is getting the drift.

I believe that this area described is in what is known as Palomas Gap. There is a place there that meets all the criteria described above. I also believe that there are between ten to twelve thousand ninety pound silver bars located there. My long-range metal detector agrees also.

In the 1930's a toll road was built through Palomas Gap to connect the community of Polomas and the railroad to the east. It was a one-way road with many parts hanging precariously close to the vertical limestone cliffs it passes through. Up to the time this road was built the only passage available was by using an ancient Spanish road that avoided the gap all together and meandered over the top then switch-backed down to the lower elevations. Today Palomas gap is one of the more remote destinations of the Caballos Mountains but well worth the effort if you have a good four wheel drive vehicle and the skill to use it. A treasure in silver could await the lucky one who eventually stumbles onto Pedro Navarrez's treasure site.

PART TWO   *THE DEPRESSION ERA*

Author's note
In part two I have tried to capture the major players from the depths of the "Great Depression" in the 1930's until the middle 1970's when the era of lawlessness finally ended on the Caballos Mountains. This was an era of desperation and struggle. Life was hard and there were no government handouts to relieve the suffering. Don't judge these people too harshly. They only did what they had to do at the time to survive.

PART TWO:

CHAPTER ONE

MRS. PERON AND THE REYNOLDS BOY

This story marks the beginning of what could be called the new era of treasure hunting in the Caballos Mountains. Although this story began during the depths of the great depression it has no bearing on the Doc. Noss story or the Palmer Brothers who both existed at about the same time this story unfolds. Doc Noss got his information directly from Geronimo while incarcerated at Fort Sill, Oklahoma but it is unknown where the Palmer Brothers acquired their information. Both were known to be successful in their endeavors on the mountain.

It all began when a young man named Jack Reynolds was hitchhiking through New Mexico. It was late at night and a storm was in progress when a man who had given Jack a ride offered to take him to some ruins that would offer him some shelter for the night. This offer Jack quickly accepted. He did not want to spend the night exposed to the elements if he had a choice.

The unnamed Samaritan took Jack to some U.S. Army ruins called Fort Sheldon, a fort that had been hastily erected shortly after the civil war and was occupied by the U.S. Calvary for a period of time when New Mexico was still a territory. Jack quickly found shelter from the rain and was soon busy looking for some dry kindling to get a fire started with. It was during this search that he found some papers stuffed in a crack in one of the walls of the fort. Upon closer inspection, Jack could see that these were detailed maps but written in Spanish. He wisely chose not to destroy them and found other material to get his fire going with.

The maps are thought to have been left by the outlaw Joaquin Joranabel, a Mexican bandit who was captured with two hundred of his men and executed by the U.S. Calvary at Fort Sheldon. This is a reasonable explanation of how the Spanish maps turned up in an English speaking fort. No one knows for sure.

Unable to read Spanish, Jack was in a quandary. What could he do to get these maps deciphered without losing them to an unscrupulous person? The answer was waiting for him less than sixty miles up the road in a town called Hot Springs.

The details of how Jack Reynolds and Mrs. Peron got together are obscure but they quickly formed a close partnership. Mrs. Peron would translate the maps while Jack Reynolds would locate the entry points. Soon there was a steady stream of gold bars coming out of the mountains carried by Jack Reynolds and disposed of by Mrs. Peron.

It is told that Mrs. Peron learned the hard way of how to dispose of gold bars. She allegedly took two gold bars to the U.S. Mint in Denver and was then told, "If you can prove that these bars belong to you we (the U.S.) will then consider paying you for them". Needless to say, no more gold bars were taken to the mint by Mrs. Peron. In those days before owning gold was illegal, it was relatively simple to find private parties to buy them or simply take the gold to Mexico and sell it. Disposing of gold became a big deal only after private ownership of gold was abolished by Teddy Roosevelt. In retrospect this law was punitive in nature and created much hardship on those fortunate enough to acquire this metal. It wasn't until President Nixon repealed this law in 1978 that American Citizens could again own Gold legally.

Most of what is known about Mrs. Peron we have John Vance to thank for. John and his twin brother spent countless hours listening to her stories about the mountain and many more hours relating them to people like me. I am certain that she walked the depths of this magical mountain and savored all of its treasures in her younger years. She was never a greedy woman and took only what she needed from the mountain.

26

Mrs. Peron and Jack Reynolds searched with good success until a tragic ending occurred. This was when an insignificant telegraph operator named Willie Doughit got wind of the maps owned by Jack Reynolds. It has never been proven because no body was ever found but Willie all but admitted to Mrs. Peron that because of him she would never see Jack Reynolds alive again. Jack's leather jacket was found with a bullet hole in the back of it in a place called Dark Canyon; a very inaccessible canyon nestled between Cable and Burbank Canyons on the Caballos Mountains.

The disappearance of Jack Reynolds ended the partnership between him and Mrs. Peron but the legacy of the maps would endure to this day. The descriptions and locations as told by Mrs. Peron have launched many a treasure hunt in the Caballos Mountains. Many of the forgotten treasure hunters owe their inspiration to the stories told by Mrs. Peron. The fact that she launched the career of Buster and Willie by indirectly providing them with vital information makes her role in the Caballos Mountain history secure. She was surely one of the good people at a time when goodness was a lost virtue.

PART TWO:

CHAPTER TWO

BUSTER AND WILLIE

Willie Doughit was a local boy born and raised under the shadow of the Caballos Mountains in New Mexico. He claimed to have been given a map by some Jesuits who wandered up from Mexico and befriended him. The probable real story is much more sinister although never proven.

Willie Doughit was a telegraph operator in Hot Springs until he found gold in the Caballos Mountains in or around 1929. In the book One Hundred tons of gold, Willie claims to have successfully located a catch on the eastern slope of the Caballos Mountains with the help of a sextant and surveyors equipment. It is commonly theorized that what Willie Doughit actually did was track James Reynolds into the mountains, shoot him in the back and then take his maps. (See my story: Mrs. Peron and the Reynolds boy) James Reynolds body was never found but his leather Jacket was found with a bullet hole in the back of it. Willie almost admitted to Mrs. Peron, that he Willie Doughit was indeed responsible for the act although it was never proven.

Willie took two newly found bars of gold and went to the hotel in Hatch, New Mexico. He had plans of going on to El Paso the following day to sell the bars. As the story goes, that night Willie was denied entry into a poker game. He was so incensed that he returned to his room and took one of the gold bars down to the poker game, tossed it on the table and said words to the effect of "If this is what I think it is, it should buy me into the poker game". Well, Willie got what he wanted and the rumors spread throughout the town of Hatch of the Gold found in the Caballos Mountains by Willie Doughit.

The next morning around 500 people showed up at the ranch where Willie had been working when the gold was found. The crowd was unruly and some even had to be forcibly removed from this previously quiet cattle ranch.

In the mean time Willie had been taken prisoner and was being tortured by his captors to force him tell where the gold was to be found. He was relieved of his gold bars, but his abductors eventually let him go after several days of torture including being hung by his scrotum with bailing wire. Willie never lost his testicles but in later years he enjoyed showing off his scrotum which hung fully eight inches lower than it should have.

Willie Doughit had learned his lesson but it was too late. Everyone knew that he had found gold in the Caballos Mountains and many were watching for him.

Willie knew that this area was too hot for him after his abduction so he went to his uncle's farm in Albuquerque to hide out for a while. It was here that Willie met Buster Ward, a cowboy who had been raised on the eastern slope of the Caballos Mountains and knew the country intimately. Buster knew the cave location just from the description given by Willie. At his first chance Buster headed for the mountain and quietly removed six bars of gold from the cave. Buster then took them to Douglas, Arizona and sold them.

Buster's luck ran out on his second trip into the Caballos Mountains when he was captured, tortured then shot and left for dead. The details of his survival are not well known but survive he did and soon a partnership was reached with Willie. Buster was to get one third of the gold by being Willies bodyguard.

In May of 1930 Buster and Willie quietly came into town at Hot Springs and borrowed the car of then judge Doan. The two quickly loaded eleven bars of gold into the car and headed west to Lordsburg where the gold was to be sold. About ten miles out of Deming, New Mexico the two were stopped by trees fallen across the road. The two were again tortured and the gold bars taken from them. During a lull in the torture, both Willie and Buster saw a chance to escape their tormentors. A Santa Fe Railroad freight train was passing close by and the two ran for it. Willie made it but Busters luck ran out. His legs hit an upright switch which threw him under the train. Both of Buster's legs were severed.

Upon seeing this happen, the abductors decided to make themselves scarce. Willie Doughit is credited with saving Buster's life by quickly applying Tourniquets to his severed legs. Buster was sitting up smoking a cigarette when help finally arrived.

Willie had one final run-in with these outlaws, two of which were reputed to be deputy sheriffs in Dona Ana County, N.M. This time their torture was effective and Willie agreed to show them the gold horde. Willie did this knowing that he had guns stashed in the cave. Upon seeing all this wealth the four assailants were so enthralled by the gold they did not see Willie slip away. Needless to say none of the four were ever seen again but both Willie and Buster had warrants issued for questioning in Dona Ana County New Mexico. These warrants were never served and the two made themselves very scarce for a while.

In 1931 both men came back to the mountain. Buster had been fitted with artificial legs and could move around almost as good as new. During the next year it is reported that the two moved about 10 truckloads of gold out of the Caballos Mountains. Both men changed their names and moved from the area. Willie was finally located in California in 1978. He made several trips back to the mountain for short periods of time. Willie died of natural causes sometime in the eighties. The exact date is unknown at this time.

It was reported in the book One hundred tons of gold, that Buster moved to Arizona and died of natural causes soon thereafter. Jerry Cheatum, the grandson of Doc. Noss reports that he located Buster in Southern California in the nineties and visited him on various occasions. It is believed that Buster is also dead of natural causes as of this writing.

As a final note both Buster and Willies estates at time of death was worth around thirty two million dollars each

PART TWO

CHAPTER THREE

DOC. NOSS

Most of what the general public knows of Doc. Noss is related to the Victorio Peak incident at White Sands Missile Range during the 1940's. Very few people know of his presence on the Caballos Mountains outside of the local who know the history of the mountain.

Doc. Noss, was a Cheyenne Indian whose real name was Milton Star. He, along with his family was moved to the Oklahoma Territory when he was a small boy. It is here where Milton grew up and at the tender age of ten years he was caught stealing a horse. Because of his age and his Indian heritage the authorities were unsure of what to do with him. He was finally sent to Fort Sill, Oklahoma where he was befriended by Geronimo who was also being held there as a prisoner of war.

Milton left Fort Sill with maps sewn into the underside of

his shirt of the Caballos Mountains and the Apache treasures buried there. These maps were not used by him until later years after he met Ova who later become his wife. Ova had just received a settlement from a previous marriage and had the means to launch a serious treasure hunt with her new husband.

Prior to this, Milton Star was apprenticed to the original Doc. Noss, a Podiatrist, at the time when this skill was considered a trade similar to dentistry. Milton Star eventually took the name of his mentor and soon became known as Doc. Noss. He set up an office in New Mexico where the laws were lax and there were plenty of people with sore feet. With this front established, Doc Noss and Ova began searching in earnest for the treasure they knew was there.

His Indian heritage served him well on the Caballos Mountains. Doc. Noss usually went to the mountain by himself for two or three days at a time taking only canned tomatoes and sardines for sustenance while packing his deadly 45 caliber pistol. He walked in and out to get the feel for the country. He would sit silently at dawn or dusk to watch the night creatures enter and exit their lairs. This is how he located most of his entrances on the Caballos Mountains. Doc. Noss always knew when he was being followed and usually the follower ended up in the bottom of a ravine or mine shaft as a reward for their efforts. Doc. Noss was a crack shot and quick to use his gun. This was a time of lawlessness on federal lands. When a stranger was met in this country one must rely upon the good will of the stranger or the quickness and accuracy of one's weapon. There was no substitute for this if you wanted to continue to live.

Doc Noss arrived here during the depths of the great depression like so many others but he was always a loner. I am sure that he knew the goings on of other treasure hunters but he never interfered with them nor did he offer to join their ranks. The other treasure hunters knew well enough not to trifle with this lean and mean stranger. Of those who did only the fortunate ones lived to regret it.

D oc. Noss strode the Caballos Mountains bigger than life. He found treasure from the old Apache maps as well as following in the footsteps of Buster Ward and Willie Doughit. What we know of Padre LaRue we learned from Doc. Noss. It was from under the hand of the body of this Jesuit priest that Doc. Noss learned of Victorio Peak and the treasure that lied there.

Doc. Noss was typical of many of the young men of his time. He would occasionally drink too much and get into trouble, then pay for it dearly later. The story is told about Doc Noss serving time for pistol-whipping a waitress in Santa Fe. I only hope it was for something worse than cold coffee. When he drank he bragged about his exploits which also caused him grievous times. Once he was captured and tortured by his assailants who burned his feet to the point that he never walked for several months after the incident.

Doc. Noss existed at a time when it was illegal to own gold. He had a lot of it but nowhere to sell it. I estimate his findings of at least four hundred bars of gold and that may be very low. He stashed the bars around the country side as the spirit moved him. To my knowledge he only trusted one person who also helped him remove gold bars. Her name was Josie Bell Butler and she accompanied him on many of his extractions.

This was before the days of four-wheel drive and Doc. Noss had an old Cadillac with eighteen-inch wheels that was almost as good as four-wheel. A small shovel and a good run on the hill usually sufficed to get him where he wanted to go.

Doc. Noss was killed in the town of Hatch, New Mexico in the late 1940's by a man named Ryan over a dispute concerning the disposal of gold bars. For those wishing to know more about this incident I would like to recommend the book "One Hundred Tons of Gold" if you are fortunate enough to find a copy. There is a loose-leaf copy of the book at the Hatch library in Hatch, New Mexico. You can read the text but you cannot remove the book. The librarians will copy all or part of it for you for a modest fee. It is well worth the time but deals mainly with Victorio Peak and the shooting incident with Ryan.

PART TWO:

CHAPTER FOUR

THE PALMER BROTHERS

Never in the history of the Caballos Mountains has such a family of cold-blooded killers ever walked the canyons of the Caballos. Jack and Reece Palmer came to the mountain during the depths of the Great Depression. Jack was the older brother and Reece the younger brother who was partially crippled. It has been said that Reece enjoyed the killings way too much and was usually the trigger man when the time came.

The reader must remember that this was during a time when extradition was unheard of. The Palmers were wanted in Sierra County, New Mexico for questioning in the disappearance of the Lars family, a husband and wife who disappeared with Eighty Thousand Dollars in cash and a lot of personal expensive jewelry. To my knowledge this was the only warrant issued and it was never served. The Palmers were from California and only came to the mountain when they needed more gold. Once they left Sierra County they were free men with no threat from law enforcement.

Typically, the Palmers would frequent one or more of the local watering holes in the community of Hot Springs. There they would carefully pick their next victim while promising wealth at a time when jobs were extremely hard to come by. The victim was kept fully supplied with whisky while the extraction took place. Once the Palmers had enough gold the victim was shot, pushed back into the hole and the entrance covered until the next time the Palmers needed gold.

No one is quite sure where the Palmers got into the mountain, at least no one who lived to tell about it. My best guess is somewhere around Granite Peak to the northeast close to the road. As you can see, very little was known about these reclusive brothers. They were a pair best to be avoided.

There was one bar in Hot Springs that stated that there were 31 disappearances unaccounted for during the Palmer Brothers era. Although 31 is an impressive number the actual number is closer to half that amount. Still an impressive record that stands to this day. As I have stated before, this was a different time and this was the last frontier so to speak. Law and order as we know it ended at the city limits. On the vast stretches of federal land there was no law enforcement except what little was provided by the local sheriffs department or by federal troops when they were in the area. It wasn't until the 1970's that the Bureau of Land Management exerted their authority and began to enforce federal law in these vast areas. Until then, one's personal safety depended upon the good will of others and one's ability to use a firearm in personal defense.

My personal estimate has the Palmers taking several hundred gold bars from the Caballos Mountains during their tenure here. Simple mathematics says that they always had an Automobile close by that was capable of carrying up to twelve hundred extra pounds. The average weight of a gold bar is from 60 to 65 pounds. Twenty bars would weigh 1200 lbs, or very close to it. Take a round number of ten trips and you have two hundred gold bars. This many gold bars would add up to a tidy sum especially during the depression years.

I do not have a good idea as to exactly where the Palmers extracted their gold but it would be reasonable to assume that they left a lot more that they took from the mountain. I have never actively searched for this treasure site because of the possibility of having to deal with bodies left by these ruthless brothers. I do believe that it is still there on the mountains but I would not envy the one who discovers this grisly treasure.

PART TWO:

CHAPTER FIVE

FRED DROLTE

Fred Drolte was a pioneer during the early days of treasure hunting in the Caballos Mountains. Fred Drolte filed numerous mineral claims on the mountain and built some of the first roads into his claims at Granite Peak. These claims were guarded with armed men paid for by Fred. Their instructions were to shoot should someone try to cross into the Granite Peak area without permission. It is certain that this did happen on occasion. Fred Drolte was able to do this because there was no Bureau of Land Management or other federal presence on the New Mexico public lands at that time. Fred Drolte was there until the mid-seventies. He mysteriously closed up his operation during that time for reasons unknown and never returned. My feeling is that he got his and left the site a happy man.

The thing about Fred Drolte's claims that make them important is that they are mineral claims filed to protect a Treasure Trove. Although this is not what the mining laws were designed to do, a mineral claim on the Caballos Mountains is usually honored by other treasure hunters as if the person filing were really after raw minerals.

One place Fred worked was particularly interesting because his driller drilled into a room that had a pile of gold bars in it. It became all the more interesting because Fred abruptly shut the operation down without attempting to recover the new finds. There were two remaining persons who witnessed this event and one of them took the drill bit to Las Cruces and had it assayed. It turned out to be around 60% gold which is consistent with the Spanish gold bars found in the area.

No one knows for sure why Fred shut down, but when he did he took very good care of the driller and the two equipment operators who were working for him at the time. It has been rumored that Fred Drolte gave each of the three $150,000 for their efforts. I think that this is more than a rumor and the three actually did receive this amount of money from Fred. I am failing to mention the names of these three at this time because two of them still remain in the area and treasure hunt on the mountain.

There is one chapter in the book "One Hundred Tons of Gold" entitled "The one armed man is king" which deals with Fred Drolte. That venerable Attorney F. Lee Bailey speaks of trouble trying to gain access to the Granite Peak claims. What his real business there was will never be known unless Bailey decides to write his memoirs.

Fred Drolte worked the mountain for over twelve years at a time when permits were not required by the BLM. A Miner with a valid mining claim could pretty much do as he or she pleased on public lands in those days and Fred Drolte was no different than other miners of his era.

It is believed in most circles that Fred Drolte removed between 80 to 150 gold bars from the Granite Peak area. How else could he afford to give his help such a generous severance pay? Fred simply did not want the responsibility of dealing with such a large find at the twilight of his career. The original hole Fred had drilled is still there on Granite Peak. It has been carefully covered up although there is about eighty feet of material accumulated in the shaft at this time. I would caution the reader not to rush to this site without obtaining the permission of the current claimants. That kind of activity is frowned upon today as much as it was fifty years ago.

The stack of gold bars Fred Drolte drilled into was rumored to be five feet high, thirty feet across and fifty feet long. These numbers have been confirmed more or less by an engineering company from Tucson, Arizona. Anyway you stack it that is a lot of gold bars.

Fred Drolte was not the last man to work the Granite Peak site. His claims were leased by three brothers who still live in the area and therefore cannot be named. Were they successful? Yes. No more can be stated at this time.

PART TWO:

CHAPTER SIX

DOC. PERRICK

Everyone who comes to the Caballos Mountains leaves an indelible mark of historical significance and Doc. Perrick was one of the more memorable ones. He wandered the mountain during the sixties and seventies, and although he never found anything of value, he is credited with destroying countless signs left by the Jesuits, the Spanish, the Aztecs and the Apaches.

Doc carried a backpack filled with explosives, which he used on a daily basis. He blasted signs off rocks and he blasted rocks to see what laid beneath and just about everything you can imagine. If Doc Perrick didn't understand something he made certain that no one in the future would be able to either. Doc. Perrick destroyed everything he didn't understand, which was a lot.

The story is told that Perrick was shot by a man named Pierce over some dispute. The same Pierce that Pierce's Cave was named after. The wound was not life threatening, however the settlement that came afterward was destructive and mean. Doc Perrick was granted permission to search Pierces Cave and he is generally regarded as the one who permanently damaged this cave. Doc blasted and probed until the cave itself was a hazard to visit. It is now filled with vertical shafts and partially caved in tunnels leading nowhere. One visit is usually enough to convince one to avoid this cave forever. It is abuse like this that has caused millions of acres of public land to be withdrawn from public entry. For those interested, the cave is easily seen from I-25 and is located at the base of the vertical limestone cliffs between Burbank and Cable Canyons.

Doc. Perrick was not a nice man and like so many treasure hunters he solicited money from investors to fund his proj-

Old Spanish mine. Photo used with permission, taken from Treasures of the Ancients, *page 196, Stephen B. Shaffer, author.*

ects. Doc's favorite method was to show potential investors some gold nuggets, then try to convince them that this was what they could expect if they invested with him. His target of choice was Senior Citizens. As a group they usually had money and usually a lot of time on their hands. Doc sold adventure and excitement and he frequently invited his investors on outings. This was simply too hard to resist for many bored retired people.

When you live by the sword you die by the sword, and for Doc Perrick this was especially true. Justice was finally served when Doc Perrick was found dead in his hotel room in Flagstaff, Arizona. He died of multiple stab wounds. Doc. had over $20,000 in possession at the time of his death and it was not taken. Robbery was certainly not the motive. Personally, I believe that the motive was revenge for some of the money taken through the years from unsuspecting investors. To my knowledge, the case was never solved.

The indiscriminate blasting and digging on public lands ended in 1978 when the Bureau of Land Management began requiring permits for this activity. This seemed to be the only thing that could stop Doc Prick from destroying the Caballos Mountains.

He has always been referred to as "Doc." But I have no information of what he was a Doctor of if indeed this was true. "Doc" Could even have been a nickname. His personal conduct certainly was not becoming of a Doctor of anything.

PART THREE

Author's note
In Part Three I have tried to include the more noteworthy personalities and events that shaped the mountain just before and after the beginning of law and order on the Caballos Mountains. No longer was one required to keep a hand on their pistol when being approached by a stranger. It is still a good idea to be armed when on the mountain but it is not essential to do so. The treasure hunters who wander there still have disagreements from time to time but these disagreements rarely end in blood shed. The Caballos Mountains are still a dangerous place to be but the dangers now are falling and breaking something, being snake bit, not enough water, heat stroke etc. etc. like most deserts in the south west.

PART THREE

CHAPTER ONE

WELLS HOVERIDE

Wells Hoveride was a major presence on the Caballos Mountains from the mid 1960's until the late 1970's. He was struck down by a debilitating disease that robbed him of his vitality and forced him to end his treasure hunting activities. Although Wells never succeeded in finding treasure he played a major role in the history of the mountain during this time period.

Wells Hoveride was the first to locate Willie Doughit and actually bring him back to the Caballos Mountains. Nothing came of the visit by Willie but it was a valiant try by Wells to gain information from a person known to have entered the mountain. It was an end run that never succeeded.

Sometimes people are better known by their misdeeds rather than their accomplishments and it wouldn't be fair to Wells Hoveride not to mention the name of Rex West in this regard. During Well's tenure on the mountain he befriended Rex West and worked with him extensively until Wells discovered that Rex was stealing information and maps that Wells had accumulated over the years. To combat this activity, Wells Hoveride began to manufacture maps on his own for Rex to steal, which he did on at least six occasions. Rex has these maps to this day and swears by their accuracy.

Stealing maps is bad but certainly not enough to be branded in history as a common thief. To his day, Rex will tell anyone capable of fogging a mirror about his last experience with Willie Doughit and Wells Hoveride. This is what Rex will be known for long after his bones are laid to rest.

On the night before Willie Doughit had agreed to show Wells Hoveride the location of a way into the mountain, Rex West went to Willie's hotel room and delivered the following message. "If any bodies are found where you will be taking us tomorrow, I will see to it that charges are filed against you for murder. I will not be a party to any of your past wrong doing." Now wasn't that brilliant? The one man alive who knew how to enter the mountain, and Rex West had just threatened him. Why didn't he wait until he was shown the entrance? Then if Rex really felt this way he could act at that time. When Rex finishes telling this story he typically turns to the listener with rapt doe eyes reeking with self righteousness and says "I wouldn't want to be a party to murder, wouldn't you do the same?" When he relayed this story to this author I could only stare at him in disbelief. The next morning Willie Doughit was on his way back to California. This has to take the all time prize for dumb! dumb! dumb! What was Rex thinking? I think if I could choose between the two I would rather be known as a common thief.

When wells Hoveride walked the canyons and ridges of the Caballos Mountains his presence was felt by everyone around him. The one thing that Wells will be remembered by most is the incident concerning burning rubber tires. Although it was a brilliantly conceived plan, it failed because one detail had been overlooked.

Wells Hoveride, in an attempt to locate hidden entrances into the mountain, burned some rubber tires inside the entrance to a natural cavern. The entrance was sealed and a large air compressor was used to move the smoke into what tunnels might exist there. The plan was brilliant but it failed. Wells sent his hired help around the area to find places where the smoke was coming out of the ground and many locations were identified.

The next day Wells gathered his troops and asked them to show him the places they had found. Bad news, nobody had taken the time to mark the exact locations and it soon became apparent that this little oversight caused the project to fail. No one could remember exactly where the smoke had emerged from the ground. This was done in Burbank Canyon at a place known as Granite Peak.

At this writing, Wells Hoveride is still alive and lucid. He resides in St. Paul, Minnesota and still enjoys a good story about the Caballos Mountains.

PART THREE

CHAPTER TWO

JOHN VANCE

John Vance is a native son of New Mexico who was born and raised in Hot Springs AKA Truth of Consequences, New Mexico. He spent his early years listening to the stories about the Caballos Mountains and much of what we know of those who came before us came from John. John knew personally Mrs. Peron, Josie Bell Butler, Doc. Perrick, The Palmer Brothers and on and on.

John is truly a fountainhead of information of which he gives freely to those willing to listen to him. He still loves a treasure hunt and like most of us know that the real treasure is the hunt itself. The effort you put into the mountain whether climbing to high places or exploring caverns is always returned to you with interest by the mountain. The gift is always there for the taking and John Vance knows this better than anyone.

John Vance has probably walked by or ignored at least ten real chances to find treasure, maybe more. Most of us may have only one or perhaps two chances to accompany someone who has already found something. John has had multiple opportunities in the past and for one reason or another they have slipped from his grasp. (See my story called Giant tables and Chairs.)

John Vance is a man who has danced through life, always with a smile and a kind word. John knows more about the Caballos

Mountains than any one living today but this is not what John is known for. John Vance is one of the more prominent artists in New Mexico. His landscapes adorn the sets of the daily television soap operas and if you were lucky enough to find one of his paintings it would be worth a lot of money.

I have always had a standing invitation to John when he comes to Truth of Consequences to join in on our excursions to the Caballos Mountains. It is always a pleasure when he finds time to join us because he brings a level of experience and expertise that none of us have.

PART THREE

CHAPTER THREE

WALLY WORLD

This is the story of Wally and his efforts to gain access into the mountain. At this writing, Wally remains unsuccessful but he is enthusiastic and undaunted in his continuing efforts to succeed.

Wally is a powder man with unorthodox methods. He blasts tiny little holes just big enough for him to fit into and normally straight down. Typically when one chances on one of his holes one almost steps in it before realizing that there is a hole there. Forty or fifty feet is nothing to this amazing man. One or two day's work is all that is necessary to accomplish this. Wally is one lean mean diggin machine.

At this writing Wally is 73 years old. I believe that he may well live to be 100 or more. I have never met a man of his age with so much energy.

I first met Wally through a mutual friend George McMullen from Canada. We were taken to Wally's, at that time,

digs on the eastern slope of the Caballos Mountains. There we found a box canyon with the most amazing group of holes and tailing piles I had ever seen. There are at least 10 holes there, all straight down. Some are 10 feet deep while others went for 100 feet or more. One of the most amazing things are the tailing piles. They are rounded and shaped like structures. If you were not standing next to them you would never recognize them for what they are; a pile of rocks.

Earlier on, George McMullen had taken Wally to this site and pointed out the exact location where the Indian Maiden disappeared into the mountain. It would have been a simple task at that time for Wally to dig a modest hole into the mountain. Wally did not completely trust George's judgment in this matter so he quickly employed the services of a local douser known as Pliers George. Pliers George used an unorthodox method of dousing using a coat hanger and a pair of pliers. Before you start to laugh at this method let me tell you that this method is just as good and effective as any other dousing method I have seen used on the Caballos Mountains, which means that it doesn't work worth a crap. I have only seen one douser who could find his or her butt with both hands and Pliers George wasn't the one. The unfortunate thing about Wally's diggings was that he collapsed the first eighteen feet of the real tunnel with his blasting in the near vicinity of the entrance.

Another unfortunate thing about this site and Wally was when Ralph Wolak used the long-range metal detector on it to determine where Wally should dig. Ralph was using the instrument in error and the readings were incorrect. Wally was so confused after the session he soon abandoned the site all together. Two years later when Ralph offered to correct his mistake, Wally had no further interest in the site.

Wally does not believe in electronic instruments. He simply feels that they are unreliable and do not work. He prefers and trusts dousing far more, and cheerfully digs hole after hole after hole. That in itself is truly amazing.

It would not be fair to write about Wally and not mention his partners. Wally is on his third partner now. Pliers George was the first and he died mysteriously. The second was one of the skinniest men I have ever seen. I don't remember his name but if he turned sideways and stuck out his tongue he would resemble a zipper. A man who was truly in need of a blood transfusion. This partner died mysteriously also. He had finger marks on his neck at the time of his death but they could have been his own. Partner Number three is currently his longest and best partnership. Ken is his name and this is a match made in heaven. Ken douses for places to dig and works diligently along side Wally while the digging is taking place. Ken believes is his dousing, as does Wally so both are happy with the arrangement. They remind me of two of the Seven Dwarfs marching off to work to dig gold and jewels from the mountain.

On a more serious note, these two are the hardest working most dedicated treasure hunters on the Caballos Mountains today. Although they have not yet succeeded, I am certain that some day they will. After all, even a broken clock is right two times a day.

Wally and Ken are active all over the Caballos Mountains but I have chosen this site for the story because I know that they have no further interest in it.

PART THREE

CHAPTER FOUR

JOHN ROMAN

John Roman was a quiet and unassuming man. He spent most of his adult life until he retired, in the community of Truth or Consequences, New Mexico. John worked at a local grocery store as a checker for over twenty years retiring in 1977.

John Roman had a secret. It all began when he acquired seven Jesuit maps. How John came about the maps is not known but one in particular was given to a woman named Annie M., a local woman who had some actual talent in map dowsing. This story is actually Annie's story because her account of John Roman is the basis of this story.

In 1976 while John was still employed by the grocery store, he came to Annie with a map and asked her to help him locate an entrance into the mountain. This she gladly did for John but she would not know the outcome of her efforts until several years later.

Several years later, it came as a surprise to Annie while she was visiting one of her friends in Las Cruces, New Mexico. The doorbell rang and John Roman was standing on the front porch. As soon as John recognized Annie, he excused himself and quickly left the area. This peaked Annie's interest and she inquired as to why John Roman would be in Las Cruces in the first place. The answer was simple; John was selling his gold bars to their mutual friend. Upon her return to Truth or Consequences, she looked up John Roman and he slowly began to confide in her.

Annie's dowsing had been extremely accurate and John had indeed located an entrance into the mountain. On the fourth level of a limestone promontory at an extremely remote location on the Caballos Mountains, John had found a circular flat area. In the middle of this flat area was an egg shaped flat rock. Upon removal of this rock a small vertical shaft descended into the mountain into a room about fifteen feet down. From this point on there were stairways descending into the heart of the mountain.

John Roman did very little exploring because he was mainly interested in the gold. He soon found a room filled with ninety pound gold bars and this was what he focused on. John was not a strong man and he was in his sixties when he made this discovery. He found that by cutting the bars in half, he could carry them out one half at a time. We know he took out at least twelve ninety pound bars and more than likely many more.

John Roman retired in 1982 and quietly moved his family back to Pennsylvania. In 1996 John passed away leaving a note to his wife to look in the garden. She must have known something about his secret because she soon unearthed twenty-four forty five pound gold bars. At this time she contacted her family members and also Annie M.

According to Annie, John Roman's son came to the Caballos Mountains and spent about one year looking for the Jesuit entrance to no avail. Annie M. still had records of her map dowsing session with John Roman and she showed me the location she had doused for John so long ago.

Annie also showed me a copy of some strange symbols that John Roman had copied off a strange object he came across while inside the mountain. The most interesting thing about these symbols is that they match the symbols of yet another object found underground in Illinois. Could these two be of the same origin? NASA believes so and is keenly interested in knowing more about these strange craft. Unfortunately there is little more to add at this time. When more is learned, another story will be told.

PART THREE

CHAPTER FIVE:

GIANT TABLES AND CHAIRS

This is a story about Mel McKinney, a treasure hunter who was successful in getting into the mountain. Just how successful he was remains a mystery to this date but I am sure that Mel found something of value before he mysteriously disappeared from the Truth or Consequences area.

Mel was a loner who trusted few and did most of his hunting alone. He also had a physical impairment, which further restricted his activities, a deformed leg that always caused him to walk with a limp. Given these two handicaps, nobody took Mel McKinney seriously.

Mel knew that he needed a reliable partner to assist him in removing gold from the mountain. For this reason Mel waited patiently in a local watering hole for three consecutive days, trying to get an audience with John Vance. John was well known at the time as a reliable treasure hunter. The John Vance story is covered in another chapter but this story wouldn't be complete without mentioning this incident.

This story occurred around 1976 when Mel McKinney was a very young man in his early twenties. John Vance at the time was spending most nights drinking and carousing with his fellow treasure hunters. (John doesn't do this anymore) The short of it was that there was something about Mel McKinney that John didn't like and he would not speak with him. Mel McKinney just rubbed him the wrong way. For three consecutive nights Mel came to the bar and John ignored him. The fourth night Mel McKinney never returned. I mention this because Mel McKinney later showed some photos around town of some very interesting objects, a table that was about five feet to the top and eight chairs that were in proportion to the table. All the items had visible gold inlay and were of remarkable artistic quality. Some of the chairs were in the position of having been recently vacated but all were fastened securely to the floor. It should be noted that there are two other accounts of these chairs. Mrs. Peron as well as Willie Doughit spoke of these giant tables and chairs and wondered about their origin. Both were known to have penetrated the secrets of the mountain and walked the silent depths of the caverns below.

Mel McKinney quietly went about his business until he had accumulated enough wealth to satisfy his future needs. Shortly before his departure from Truth or Consequences, New Mexico, Mel was seen driving in a brand new pickup truck. It was jokingly suggested that Mel had hit big on the mountain. Mel's reply was"if I did, I did it the right way". Mel quietly left town and has never been seen again in central New Mexico. It is rumored that he is living somewhere in Texas under an assumed name.

For those of you who are interested in where Mel McKinney got in the mountain, there are several rumors. The first one is that he got in somewhere at the top of Longbottom Canyon. There are lots of caves there and some are homes for rattlesnakes so beware. The second one is somewhere on the eastern slope of the Caballos Mountains in an area called brushy mountain. I have even heard that there are two rock carvings of Spanish solders in armor at the cave entrance. Remember, I am reporting rumors. No one but Mel McKinney knows for sure where he went into the mountain.

PART THREE

CHAPTER SIX

ANGELS LANDING

A ngels landing is a name given a promontory of limestone that separates Burbank Canyon from Longbottom Canyon in the Caballos Mountains of New Mexico. It can be reached most easily by driving up to the communication towers from the Joranado Del Muerto to the east of the mountain range. The road is good and the vehicle can be parked at the top with relative safety from thieves and vandals.

"Angel's landing" provides spectacular views of the Caballos area. Photo ©, William H. White.

One must then hike south to the roads end which is about one eighth of a mile of easy walking. From this point on the trail is not for the weak, lazy or over weight. You start down hill almost immediately with a combination of light rock climbing and careful walking until the bottom of the trail is reached. The trail from this point on is easily followed; continuing in a southerly direction until one emerges onto a relatively flat area at the upper reaches of the limestone cliffs that dominate the scenery when viewed from the canyon below. This is the area loosely referred to as Angels landing.

The trail branches at this point with the left trail heading for Hidden Valley, a pleasant remote place littered with truck sized boulders broken off from the cliffs above. This valley is about two miles from the trail fork and well inside Burbank Canyon, a worthy destination for those who love remote places and privacy.

The trail fork to the right is the one that will take the hiker to Angels Landing and the Hurley Claims. This story is about George Hurley, a man who lived and died with an obsession and who was never successful in his attempts to find his way back into the mountain that he had seen when he was a lad of seventeen.

George was a local boy who grew up under the shadow of the Caballos Mountains. He was befriended by an Apache Indian who was rumored to be a relative of Geronimo. This Indian, whose name is unknown, took George into the mountain through an opening somewhere on the face of the limestone cliffs close to Angels Landing. George was quite young at the time and it wasn't until he was in his early forty's that he began in earnest to try to regain entrance into the mountain.

There is an enclave, or horizontal indentation on the limestone cliffs and this is where George established his base camp. The trail starts down steeply from the ridge back to this location and ends up with a forty-foot vertical climb, which I recommend only for experienced rock climbers. One slip would mean a seven hundred foot fall to the canyon floor below.

56

George Hurley was never able to locate the original hole he entered with the Indian so many years ago. George did what most obsessed men on the Caballos Mountains did; he started blasting holes into the mountain to try to intercept the cavern he knew existed somewhere close. The hole was done with an economy of assets. It is about four feet high and two feet wide and it stretches for about one hundred and fifty feet into the mountain. It is very cramped and dangerous due to lack of shoring but worth seeing for those few adventurous enough to reach the enclave.

PART FOUR

Author's note
In Part Four of this writing I have selected some of my favorite treasure stories of the Caballos Mountains. Some are merely adventures while some have real prospect of fruition. The reader must be the judge of this. The real joy of treasure hunting is the anticipation of succeeding. We are a strange lot we treasure hunters. We get up each morning feeling that today is our birthday and before the day is through we will receive presents. If it doesn't happen today, that is all right because there is always tomorrow to look forward to. If we walk into a room full of horse dung we always look for the pony. We are the world's greatest optimists.

CHAPTER ONE

ACE'S HIDEOUT

This story is actually about a military installation that may exist in and on the Caballos Mountains. It began with a phone call from a retired Army Colonel whose name is not important. The call was made at the request of Wells Hoveride, a long time friend of he Colonel.

The call came in on our cell phone one afternoon while we were working in Longbottom Canyon. The Colonel explained that his last duty before retiring from the Army was to inspect the military facilities that exist on the Caballos Mountains.

As the story goes, the Colonel drove to the towers from the east side using the service road. From there he went south along a steep trail to a point where the trail divided. The trail to the right went to Angels Landing while the less used trail to the left went to the military facility. The Colonel described it as a concrete bunker with a chain link fence around it. According to the Colonel, the chain link fence had been breached with a ladder and people had been going inside the facility.

The Colonel proceeded to enter the bunker and descend for four levels at which point a massive iron door with a monster padlock in place. The Colonel had a key.

From here he descended six to eight levels until he came to the storage areas the Army had seen fit to supply in the early years following World War II. Our Colonel's job was to inventory the items left by the military and make sure that nothing had been pilfered over time. I can give you a rough sketch of what was there as told by the Colonel but I cannot be specific. There were chemical agents, water and food, gold bullion and two flying machines. Nothing had been touched or pilfered at this inspection so the Colonel reported. I thanked him for the information and terminated the call.

Could this possibly be true? John Roman had reported seeing these machines, as did Willie Doughit. Could these be the same machines they observed when passing through the mountain?

According to the Colonel this was designed as a safe haven for our scientists and statesmen in times of national crisis. America had moved into the Atomic Age at the close of WWII and at that time no one actually knew how things would turn out in the future. The Army was just improving their survival position in an era of uncertainty

I call this story Ace's hideout because there was a rumor around town that Ace, a local character, had located this bunker and went up there to play survivalist from time to time. Other than that there is no connection. I have never met Ace and I am unsure if he is still around town.

I have searched for this bunker on at least eight occasions and never found it at this writing. I believe it to be in upper Burbank Canyon somewhere near Sardine Canyon for those interested in helping search for it. What troubles me is the unsolicited phone call from The Colonel. Why would he call me if this weren't true? There was absolutely no reason for him to deceive me. We have never met.

According to the Colonel, the Army is aware of this facility but it is just on a back burner for the time being. The day may come when the Army will come and remove this facility if they have not already done so.

PART FOUR

CHAPTER TWO

BAT CAVE

Bat Cave entrance. Photo courtesy ©, Ralph Wolak.

One of the more prominent features on the western slope of the Caballos Mountains is an enormous hole that opens like a cornucopia or more like the flair of a trumpet. Bat Cave is situated on the southern vertical limestone face of Cable Canyon and is easily seen when driving northbound on I-25 in the early afternoon.

Both Doc Noss and Mrs. Peron spent a lot of time and energy here in days gone by. Both claimed that there was an easy access into the mountain somewhere around bat cave.

Leaving Bat Cave, Lewis Jameson and William White, photo ©, courtesy of Ralph Wolak.

This is what brought us to the cave. Ralph Wolak, Lewis Jameson and I all agreed that we should try our new ground penetrating radar on the cave floor in the hope of finding a concealed entrance into the mountain.

The road into Cable Canyon is rough but passable and soon we were at roads end looking up into the yawning mouth of bat cave. Nobody realizes how intimidating the mouth of this cave can be when observed from just below. We had set our goals on a trip to Bat Cave and that was going to happen regardless of how we felt when first arriving. No one bought up the subject of quitting the hunt.

The three of us were carrying substantial loads and the trail is quite steep up to the mouth of the cavern. We soon fell into a rhythm and were at the final assault within the hour. This was when a moment of truth was at hand. There was forty feet of vertical limestone before us with no safety ropes. One slip would mean disaster.

I was the most experienced rock climber and therefore volunteered to scale the cliff and determine if the climb was doable for my two companions. I left my backpack and soon discovered an easy route to the entry point. A rope was lowered and I pulled the backpacks up while the other two quickly climbed into the cave.

The cave had been excavated in days gone by and less than fifty feet into the cave a vertical shaft dropped down fifty feet or more. This was a hole to be avoided because a fall in there would be as disastrous as a fall down the rock face outside.

We set up our equipment and soon went to work on the horizontal floor of Bat Cave. The floor is covered with Guano so the cave is aptly named. The results were inconclusive but after one and one half hours of shooting the radar a possible entrance location was chosen. Let me stress that there was only an outside chance that a hole existed.

We had brought one shovel, which we quickly put to work taking turns as the digging progressed. After two feet it became apparent that we were digging in previously undisturbed soil. No secret entrance here, just a bunch of compacted rocks, dirt and bat stuff. It was becoming clear to all of us that this project was coming to a conclusion. There was nothing here of interest for us but we were secure in the knowledge that we had given it the old college try or something like that.

We broke for a quick lunch but no one was willing to bring up the subject that was on all of our minds. Getting out of here without tumbling to our death was going to be a real challenge. The problem is that the bat cave slopes down to the vertical and there are no hand holds at the moment of descent onto the vertical face. Whether I liked it or not, I was volunteered to ascend first.

In case I died trying to get out of this cave let me say that the view is truly stunning from this vantage point. It is definitely a Kodak moment of moments and well worth the trouble to get there.

I gingerly moved to the vertical face and slowly lowered my legs over the precipice. I remembered that there were indeed foot holds down there if I could only find them. I slowly began sliding down the slope while frantically groping for anything like a hand or foothold. There was no point of complaining now. When I accepted the role of the most experienced climber I inherited the role of being the first off the mountain. As I have said many times, a coward dies a thousand deaths and this was no time to waver. The reader has probably guessed by now that I didn't die and actually found a substantial foot hold moments before my momentum carried me out of control.

I remained at this location and guided my other two companions off the mountain then lowered the backpacks to the talus slope below. We were soon back to our vehicle and headed down the mountain. We all agreed that we had been unable to solve the riddle of Bat Cave but we all had a memorable experience. Let me caution the reader that ascending into Bat Cave requires some experience in rock climbing, but descending from Bat Cave requires even more experience.

I would recommend this climb for anyone capable of it. It is truly an experience to be remembered.

PART FOUR

CHAPTER THREE

CABALLO CAVE

The Caballo Cave is located about one mile south of Palomas Gap at the end of an old Spanish road. From this roads end there is a trail up the wash and over the top to the adjoining wash to where the cave actually lies.

This is a story of a trip made into the bowels of this cave by four senior citizens with the hope of finding a way into the heart of the mountain.

Ralph Wolak, Jim Neideg, Lewis Jameson and I all met for breakfast the morning of our planned departure into this cave. Of all of us only Lewis Jameson had experience with this cave and of the four of us, Jim Neidig and myself were the two most experienced rock climbers. Ralph Wolak was the least experienced but made up the difference in enthusiasm. It was an adventure that all of us had looked forward to in the days of planning preceding this event.

Because of the amount of gear we were planning to carry into the cave we needed two vehicles to get us to the trailhead. It was ten o'clock in the morning when we finally started up the trail. The packs carried food and water for three days plus many supplies we would all need while in the cave. The average pack weighed around fifty pounds. This seemed more like one hundred pounds as the trail steepened. The climb was uneventful which means that nothing bad happened. At one point the trail becomes so steep there is nothing but rock to walk up. The angle of ascent is low enough to allow walking with feet while hands are placed on the rock above. If it were any steeper we would have needed safety ropes.

We peaked at the top and completed the short walk around the mountain to the mouth of the cave. It was time to rest and regain our lost electrolytes before descending into the dark hole below us. Lewis Jameson happily informed us that we had made the climb almost twenty minutes earlier than the average person, a small victory for those of us over fifty.

The mouth of the cave had bars over the entrance and the usual BLM disclaimers and warnings. At one time the entrance was locked but the locks were always cut by the spelunkers coming here. The government finally decided to give up replacing them.

We quickly moved into the mouth of the cave and adjusted our equipment for the trek into the mountain. Lewis Jameson led the way because he had been here before. The main room is quite large and slopes downward in a northeastern direction for about three thousand yards until abruptly terminating with truck sized boulders. The walking becomes extremely dangerous from this point on until reaching our dissension hole. Here again the BLM graciously left a sign telling us to proceed no further. It was very kind of them to mark the hole for us and eliminated search time on our part in finding it.

We were certainly were not the first ones into this cave but as we descended into the mountain deeper and deeper, fewer and fewer graffiti signs marked the walls. We were getting to the point that separates the men form the boys in cave exploring and we all knew it.

Typically, we would descend into a level then pass the backpacks down on ropes to the level below. After all were accounted for, we would begin a search of the surrounding caves looking for a passage to penetrating ever downward.

We had been climbing steadily for about six hours when we were finally stymied. The passage was simply too small to continue. On a positive note we were able to actually see the floor of the main cave below us from about thirty feet up but no one was successful in finding a way down to it. It was reluctantly decided by all to turn around and begin out ascent out of this cave.

Moving upward was just as arduous as descending. One person had to go up and station himself at a point where he could lift the back packs and place them out of the way so the other three could join him. This pattern was repeated time and time again until we all finally emerged at the main room. It was now 10:30 at night. We had been steadily climbing for over ten hours but it didn't seem near that long to any of us.

We had all lost serious body fluid during this climb and we needed to refresh ourselves and get some rest. Jim Neidig found a relatively flat area close to the surface and we soon began to unwind and try to get some sleep. We were all exhausted but still wired by the excitement of the adventure. It was several hours until any of us could actually begin to drift off to sleep.

I always pack a gun when on the mountain and this was no exception. It was safely stashed within easy reach. Lewis Jameson was also armed in like manner. I was just ready to fall asleep when I heard footfalls. Someone was in the cave with us! Needless to say, both Lewis and I went ballistic immediately with our flashlights and guns in hand. There was no one there. After a thorough search nothing moved inside the cave. Both of us agreed that what we actually heard were footfalls. This mystery had no apparent explanation. We finally settled down and tried to drift off to sleep once more.

Later that night with both Ralph Wolak and Jim Neidig sound asleep we had a parade. It lasted for over ten minutes and there were big ones and small ones crunching along on the cave gravels. Both Lewis Jameson and I laid there fully awake and calmly listened to this without responding. The next morning we talked about this and both agreed that whatever it was we both felt safe and that there was no cause for alarm.

That same morning Lewis Jameson suggested that we had been visited by Big Foot the night before. This would also explain the horrid smell both of us noticed during the night. Why we couldn't see them is a mystery to me as well as why I allowed intruders to march by my sleeping place without becoming alarmed. I would recommend that the reader find some books on the mysterious Sasquatch that may explain some of this phenomenon. I just don't know.

The next morning we all quickly scrambled through the bars and made ready to descend to the trailhead below. Within an hour we were down and had to wait for our ride back to town. We were tired but it had been a rewarding experience for all of us. Although we had not located an entrance into the mountain we had all profited immensely by the attempt. I would recommend this cave to any experienced spelunker. It is well worth the effort expended to get there.

PART FOUR

CHAPTER FOUR

CARLOTTA'S CROWN

Not many are familiar with this tale and how it intertwines with the Caballos Mountains but like all of the stories in this book it is based on fact and credible witnesses. Carlotta's Crown is no different from so many tales except that it involves Mexico, Napoleon and Maximilian.

At the time when the French forces under the Emperor Napoleon were rampaging though Europe, Napoleon decided to extend his influence into the new world. Deep down in his guts he knew that eventually he would rule the world so why not jump-start the process in Mexico? To this end Napoleon installed Maximilian of Austria and his wife Carlotta as the king and queen of Mexico. To ensure this end, Napoleon left a formidable army in Mexico City.

Maximilian and Carlotta moved into the imperial palaces in Mexico City and made themselves at home. There were once again Europeans dictating to the Mexican people. The Mexicans hated it but felt at the time that nothing could be done about it. And so it was until the time came when the war in Europe started going bad for Napoleon.

As you may have expected, Napoleon promptly withdrew his troops who were desperately needed elsewhere. Maximilian and Carlotta would just have to fend for themselves. Those of you who think that the French habit of abandoning their troops and friends is something new should consider that it was done in the time of Napoleon also. As in Algiers and Vietnam where the French later were to leave their troops to die, so in like manner did Napoleon leave these people to the wrath of the Mexicans. Only the palace guard was left to defend the Maximilian's. How utterly French. How utterly hopeless.

Knowing that the end was near, Maximilian quickly gathered his treasures and sent them north with Carlotta in an attempt to reach New Orleans and hopefully passage back to Austria. Maximilian himself remained behind to stall the attackers and direct the defense of the palace. On what was to become the Mexican Independence Day, Cinco De Mayo, (the fifth of May) the attackers successfully stormed the palace and Maximilian was put to death. This ended once and for all the European intervention in Mexico.

Meanwhile, Carlotta was safely on her way when disaster struck at a place now known as Castle Rock Texas. There her small party was attacked by a well-coordinated force of Apache Indians. Only Carlotta herself managed to escape the massacre.

Carlotta eventually appeared in Yuma, Arizona (a sea-port at the time) and was given a paupers passage back to Europe. She lived out her days in seclusion and died of old age in Austria.

Maximilian treasure was split up among the Chiefs, one of whom happened to be the famous Apache Chief Victorio. Victorio had no real use for this booty so he took it to what is now known as White Sands New Mexico. There is a place there that was to become known as Victorio Peak. It was in the tunnels and caves beneath this mountain that Chief Victorio stashed his treasure and among the items taken that day in Texas was Carlotta's Crown. Here it remained until our famous treasure hunter Doc Noss appeared on the scene with information gleaned from under the dead hand of Padre LaRue.

I have seen photographs of this crown. It has over two hundred diamonds and two large pigeon blood rubies on it. It is quite spectacular even in a photograph. This photograph was taken by Ova Noss (Doc's wife at the time) and was in the possession of Jerry Cheatum, Ova's grandson.

Doc Noss brought the crown back to Hot Springs, New Mexico and left it in his house. During this time, Ova cleaned the crown and eventually took it down to the local butcher shop and had it weighed on the butcher scales. This proved to be a major mistake because when Doc Noss heard of it he became incensed. So angry was he that he loaded up all things the family held valuable into a metal trunk and left with them. Upon his return he would only say that he had buried the valuables in Ash Canyon. The Crown has never been seen since.

Many a search has been conducted in The Ash Canyon that runs behind Turtleback Mountain to no avail. Personally I have never thought that the Crown was there. There is another Ash Canyon in Longbottom Canyon and I feel that it is stashed somewhere near there. I feel that the Crown is on or in the mountain somewhere. It, like so many other treasures is out there waiting for the right one to come along and claim their prize.

So put on your good hiking boots, stow some trail mix in your back pack and take lots of water and a quality metal detector and get to work. Carlotta's Crown is out there waiting for someone and it may be you.

PART FOUR

CHAPTER FIVE

CRYSTAL CAVE

This story begins around 1980 in the town of Truth or Consequences, New Mexico, and is ongoing as of this writing. For this reason, I am not including the last names of the participants of this story.

Jeremy who was nine years old at the time was deer hunting with his father around an area known as Polomas Gap in the Caballos Mountains. While they were sitting in a deer stand searching the terrain for animals, Jeremy noticed an opening in the rock formation they were adjacent to. Being an inquisitive lad, Jeremy wiggled through the opening and came into a very large cavern that stretched for about 4000 feet or more and gently downward into the earth. Jeremy didn't have much time to enjoy his find because his father became upset with concern for his son's safety. Out came Jeremy and the incident was soon forgotten by his father. Jeremy however, didn't forget this new-found cave.

Back at school the next day, Jeremy soon recruited two friends to help him explore the cavern, John who was twelve and Otis who was fifteen. The date was set for the next Saturday morning.

When Saturday came around the three explorers were up early and headed toward the Caballos Mountains. The Rio Grande River was low so they waded across carrying their bicycles, then off they went. They were well equipped for this adventure. They had a sack full of candy bars and only one flashlight between the three of them. No one was concerned that there were no extra batteries. It was about a six mile ride from town to where they wanted to go but they were young and filled with excitement. They soon arrived at their destination.

Jeremy although the youngest, had the best sense of direction and had little trouble finding the cavern. Within two hours their adventure would really begin.

The three entered the cavern and began slowly moving to the back while marveling at the various crystals that adorned the passageway. They soon discovered an even easier access into a far larger cavern at the far end and away they went. The three adventurers didn't know it at the time but they had just entered the fabled inside of the Caballos Mountains.

They reported that the floor was smooth and sometimes they walked abreast twenty five feet apart as they journeyed into the bowels of the mountain.

Eventually, they began to encounter burials with mummies and skeletons. This development had the effect of terrifying the boys but by now they had little choice but to keep moving and hope that an exit would be found before their flashlight expended its batteries. The boys estimated later that they walked almost six miles but I have reason to believe that it was closer to nine miles.

The adventurers eventually reached an area containing many caskets hastily deposited and stacked. One casket had inadvertently come open and Jeremy quietly removed a golden goblet from the interior. I have seen this goblet and it is inscribed Padre Latrado (a Jesuit priest from the 1600's).

There is also a river inside this mountain and only Jeremy had the courage to wade it to get a closer look at the rooms on the other side. Jeremy reported that these rooms were filled with gold bars with a crown emblem on them. This symbol usually meant that this treasure was destined to the coffers of the King of Spain.

The Jesuits were thrown out of the new world for their failure to pay the kings taxes. This treasure was likely stashed here to prevent paying those taxes.

The flashlight was growing dim and time was running out for the three boys. They had to find a way out soon or they would surely perish in this dark under world. Jeremy came to the rescue once again, he noticed that there was a breeze coming from one of the passageways and suggested that the trio make a run for it down this passage in the hope that an exit could truly be found.

Once again, Jeremy's luck held up. When the three came to the end of the passageway, three rocks were moved and out they went into the night air. A road was soon located and these three actually ran back to their bicycles nine miles away.

Upon arriving home the three got into the usual trouble kids do at that age, and they all promised never to go into the mountain again.

This is a nice story, however it does not end here. I first learned of this cave while talking to Otis, the oldest of the three but now a hopeless drug addict still living in Truth or Consequences.

I became fascinated with the story and soon asked Otis to show me this cave, which he promised to do the next day. When the next day rolled around, Otis was suffering from the perpetual drug hangover that addicts have to endure. Needless to say he was in no mood to show anybody anything. It took me several attempts before I came to realize that Otis would never show anyone the cave because it was his only source of self-esteem, or he had simply forgotten the location..

One of my associates was able to locate John, the twelve year old who shared their adventure twenty years before. John was helpful but could not remember where he was at that time. John eventually put my associate in touch with Jeremy.

Now Jeremy was living in Albuquerque at the time and running a small printing company. At first Jeremy did not want to talk about the cave but he soon warmed up and began to speak about his experiences. We learned that Eddie and his girlfriend had been in the cave five years prior. His girlfriend had walked into a room full of human skulls and became frightened. They had to leave immediately.

Up to this point, Jeremy had shown no interest in the treasure lying beneath the mountain. Little did we know that Jeremy would again show his ability to get what he wanted and disappear without a trace.

Jeremy had quietly sold his business, packed his clothes and vanished with his girlfriend in tow. He made one mistake however and this mistake brought him back to the mountain.

Jeremy and his girlfriend had removed approximately four million dollars of gold from the   caverns. They had taken it to Mexico, sold it and headed for the Virgin Islands.

Jeremy's mistake was that he only took four million dollars worth of gold. After buying a condo and a respectable boat to float around in, he gave his relatives much more money than he should have; Jeremy was broke again.

I will end this story by saying that Jeremy did come back to the mountain and this time he took enough wealth to last him for a year of two. I can say no more about Jeremy.

PART FOUR
CHAPTER SIX

GALLEGOS HOLE

Gallegos Hole is a name given a prominent natural opening on the eastern slope of the Caballos Mountains. Only one hole is visible from above but in reality there are three holes that disappear into the earth from that location.

In the 1960's a man by the name of Mike Gallegos had a cabin near this hole and several mineral claims in the surrounding public land. This was before the Bureau of Land Management had a significant presence in this area. Mike had good reason to believe that there was treasure buried nearby and this was his real reason for being here. Mike was systematically searching the surrounding countryside for signs of what he believed to be a Spanish treasure trove.

Mike Gallegos had two nephews who had come to spend the summer with their uncle. Because of their age Mike gave them the run of the mountain, a very healthy sensible thing to do at the time. Certainly there was no harm in letting the boys explore the area. At least this is what Mike thought.

These two adventurers eventually located Gallegos Hole and began to explore it. The two carefully climbed down almost 60 feet when the cavern opened up horizontally into a large room. One of the youths began to feel sick and went no further but his brother had no such symptoms and continued on into the tunnel. He called to his brother saying that he could see piles of gold bars and stacked rifles, then the sickness hit him as he attempted to make his way back to where his brother was waiting.

The adventurous one got back to where his brother waited then collapsed, overcome by what he had inhaled in the cavern. Being unable to climb out while carrying his brother, the first one scrambled for the surface and went for help. The brother remaining below was found dead when help finally arrived, and the other brother died about six months later after a lingering illness. As for Mike Gallegos, he was grief stricken, and as a safety precaution, set off a charge to partially fill in the cavern where the boy had died. As you would have guessed, he overdid the charge and filled the cavern up to about twenty-five feet to the surface.

The word soon got out about what the brothers has said about the hole. Mike was approached by an exploration group from California called "Triangle Corp." who offered to clear the rubble and explore the cave with the hope of locating the gold bars and rifles the boy spoke of. Mike Gallegos agreed and the Triangle Corp. hired Jack Vance to head up the digging activities. The digging was going well and they were approaching 45 feet when someone complained of a headache. This was all that was needed to shut down the dig. Jack Vance immediately stopped the dig and to my knowledge no other digging has been done since. Mike Gallegos abandoned the east side all together and for a time worked in Pierce's Cave, then disappeared from the mountain altogether.

I believe this treasure to be there but I also am convinced that it will be extremely dangerous to extract. Most knowledgeable treasure hunters attribute the poisonous gas to cyanide that Geronimo was known to possess. I do not agree with this theory for two reasons. Soil contaminated with cyanide usually turns a sickly reddish color and there is none of that in or around Gallegos Hole. Secondly, a far more insidious gas could be present which would more likely cause the symptoms experienced by the two cousins. Arsenic is a common substance found around gold bars especially Dore bars that contain only 65% pure gold with the balance being non-ferrous metals. It is odorless and in a confined space over time could build up into lethal doses to those who happen in on it. The solution is to simply purge the air because lethal doses of this gas take much time to accumulate.

This site is hard to get to and harder to work but for those hardy enough and with large enough huevos to risk the gas, it is there waiting for you.

PART FOUR

CHAPTER SEVEN

MISSION OF THE SEVEN DOLORES

This is another treasure story that happens to be located about a half mile to the north of this Mission. The Mission is only a pile of stones now but at one time it was a vibrant Jesuit mission located above the eastern rim of Burbank Canyon. The Mission of the Seven Gardens was its name. After visiting the site the question is always raised; where did these Jesuits get

INTERIOR OF MISSION CHURCH.

their water? This is a real mystery. Surely the Padres didn't carry the water up by mule. The answer is always pure speculation. I believe that there were underground resources available that are no longer visible. This mission, along with eight others were hastily closed by the Jesuits and later razed by the marauding Indians during the 1680 Pueblo Revolt. Like the other eight missions, it was never reopened.

About one half of a mile north from these ruins, I have good reason to believe that there is a substantial treasure cache buried.

In the 1950's, there is a story of a Shepherd who was grazing his sheep along the eastern slopes of the Caballos Mountains. After dinner one evening he dropped down onto a ledge to shelter from the wind while lighting a cigarette. As he hunkered down he noticed a small opening and what could be a stairway descending into the mountain.

That night he could think of nothing else and the next morning he decided to explore this find. As with all who live in and around this mountain, he had heard many stories of the riches that the mountain contained.

After a short time the sheepherder soon had the hole big enough to crawl into. Armed with only a flashlight, he slowly descended the stairs to the room below. He was not disappointed. In the room at the bottom of the stairs was a stack of three hundred gold bars. The Sheepherder examined them then ascended back to the surface taking nothing with him.

Our Sheepherder was a simple man who had lived his life quietly on the slopes of the mountains with only his sheep for company. After thinking it through, the shepherd decided that this was not a bad life after all. He was deeply concerned that this new wealth would propel him into a life he may not like and once committed, there would be no turning back. Why not just leave the treasure where he found it and continue on as he was before? This was a life he understood and enjoyed. Why change it now?

78

The story became known because our shepherd loved to bend an elbow and loved equally a good story. When he would come into Hot Springs for supplies he always stopped at the local watering hole for refreshments. The subject always came up about his treasure-find and his story never wavered. There were many who didn't believe him because they had difficulty with the fact that he just walked away from this treasure without taking even one gold bar. Believe it or not, some people really are that way.

We eventually located the shepherd's old campsite by the descriptions others had left, and proceeded to explore the area with our electronic equipment. In little time we had located a cave within ten feet of the surface and a precious metal hit at around sixty feet down. This confirmed the shepherd's descriptions. No entrance has been found at this writing but the cave is close to the surface. This is one of the many projects we have yet to complete on the Caballos Mountains. So many treasures, so little time.

PART FOUR

CHAPTER EIGHT

THE FLOWER OF CARMEL MINE

The Flower of Carmel Mine was one of those mines that was so rich the Spaniards placed an iron door over the entrance to keep casual inspections from occurring. It exists in the Caballos Mountains to this date, but has not been active since the 1680 Pueblo Revolt. After the hasty retreat of the Spaniards, it washed out by flash floods.

The first we knew of this mine were confidential reports by Doc Noss telling of layers of gold hanging from the walls and

ceilings. This report was later verified by Josie Bell Butler at her deathbed testimony to her relatives.

The first official name given this site was from the deceased Don Fingado who saw references of this mine in the old records in Madrid, Spain. It was he who gave the mine its name, or returned the name to the mine as given by the Spanish.

Doc Noss and Josie Bell both spoke of an iron door partially caved in from the front with large boulders blocking the entrance from the outside. This mine was observed from the inside not the outside at a time when the two were removing gold bars from the area.

Both Buster Ward and Willie Doughit observed this mine and reported similar findings. They had no interest in working it because so many gold bars lay around for the taking. It must have been nice.

The Flower of Carmel Mine is in Longbottom Canyon about half way up between the top and the bottom of canyon itself. It rests below a six foot outcropping of black basalt and the entrance faces due north.

I have shot it with my long-range metal detector with good results and ran underground radar over it with mixed results. It is there, I have no doubt, but how deep it is and how many obstructions must be removed, I am unsure.

It would have to be dug by hand due to the steep terrain for those interested in this kind of thing. The site is also under claim at this time as a mineral claim. How long this will last who can tell? The present claimant is not interested in this mine because he does not know that it is there.

PART FOUR

CHAPTER NINE

THE INDIAN MAIDEN TREASURE

This story occurred around the turn of the century at the Caballos Mountains. The amazing thing about this story is that it concerns a small band of Cherokee Indians who were moved to the mountain by the Federal government some time around 1900. There are many tales of Indians of other tribes but to my knowledge this is the only story concerning Cherokee transplants from Louisiana.

The mother's name was Yellow Flower and her daughter's name was Morning Star. This writing concerns the observations of Morning Star when she was ten years old and taken through the mountain by the tribal shaman.

The story begins with the urgent need to join the tribe which was gathering food at the time in what is now known as Burbank Canyon, on the western slope of the Caballos Mountains. The reasons for haste are long forgotten but due to the nature of the emergency the tribal shaman took Yellow Flower and her daughter to an entrance on the eastern slope of the mountain. This entrance is situated in a box canyon where the limestone wash abruptly changes to vertical cliffs. This cannot be observed unless one is standing at the base of the cliffs due to the foliage blocking the upper view. You simply have to walk up on it to recognize that it is a natural box canyon. The entrance into the mountain lies here, although the first eighteen feet have been collapsed by indiscriminate blasting done by Wally. The amazing feats of this man are more fully covered in the story Wally World which covers this same area.

The shaman instructed Yellow Flower that what she was

about to see must remain a tribal secret forever. According to the shaman, the treasure within the mountain was inherently evil and harm would befall the Cherokee in the event that any gold bars were taken. With that being said, the two were quickly shown the entrance and moved into the mountain. The entrance was small and sharply turned to the right after about ten feet. The cave widened at that point and it was easy walking from then on.

The cave was cool compared to the afternoon sun they had just left and soon they were moving at a good pace with just the light from a home made torch to guide them. The party soon began passing a series of rooms that were stacked with Spanish Dore bars thrown in like firewood. This display continued for a very long time until the three had almost reached the exit in Burbank Canyon.

Buster Ward and Willie Doughit both reported a similar description of this tunnel in later observations but never went after it because there were far easier catches located closer to the surface and roads. This place was far more remote at the time.

Yellow Flower was content with the world she found herself in. Everything the tribe needed was provided by the Rio Grande and surrounding countryside. Yellow Flower truly felt that she and her tribe were surrounded by abundance. Morning Star, who was ten years old at the time, didn't agree with her mother.

Morning Star had observed at an early age that the white settlers lived much better than the Indian. She simply never understood why the tribe didn't take some of the gold and improve their lives with it. It just didn't make sense to her.

Morning Star attended school and eventually became a nurse. She married a local person and had two children. Morning Star never went back to the mountain tunnel she had been to as a child. In her waning years she tried to instruct her children where the entrance was but the landmarks were long gone and the children were unsuccessful in their attempts to locate this place. Morning Star lived out her life and died within the shadow of this magnificent mountain, never venturing too far away.

The last person who gave a description of this quarter mile of gold was Doc Noss who also felt that there were easier places to remove treasure than this tunnel. I think that it's there to this day. I also think that this was a principle location for the Apaches who gave back to the earth what the Spaniards had taken. The gold and silver bars were always removed after a successful raid and the Caballos Mountains were a natural storage area that the Apaches knew well.

PART FOUR

CHAPTER TEN

THE IRON HORSE TREASURE

Geronimo had a son named Iron Horse. Although he was never famous like his father, he was a warrior of note within the Apache community. Like so many Apaches of

his time when the war against the European invaders was being waged, Iron Horse stored much of his booty on the Caballos Mountains. This is one such story of his treasure location and of those who searched for it in later years.

The treasure is known on the Caballos Mountains as the Cowboy Silver Bar Treasure, and is located within the confines of Burbank Canyon. This story is about the treasure search, not about Iron Horse. There is too little information that exists about him.

The story occurs during the 1930's and 1940's at a time when the Caballos Mountains were wild and dangerous. A cowboy whose name is unimportant would make a pilgrimage into Burbank Canyon about once per month. After each visit the cowboy would return with a ninety pound silver bar in his possession. This silver bar would be quickly taken to Las Cruces and disposed of. The net to the cowboy was around $250.00, a tidy sum in those days. It was certainly a comfortable amount to live on during those tough times.

The cowboy was followed many times but soon the trail would become extremely hazardous and most would turn back. The cowboy always entered from the eastern slope of the Caballos Mountains, going over the rim and traversing the talus slope below the sheer cliffs to his secret destination. Nobody ever found out where the cowboy was getting his silver but for many years, once a month the cowboy came and went on the Caballos Mountains. Eventually, the cowboy died and left no clue as to the location of this treasure. Because it was silver and not gold, there was only lukewarm interest in finding it. The treasure was talked about around campfires but no one seriously searched for it.

Those who did search for it normally confined their search area to the upper cliffs of Burbank Canyon. As I was to find out, that is much too high. This treasure actually rests mid-canyon around the cliffs adjoining Sardine Canyon. I also have reason to believe that there are a substantial amount of gold bars buried at the same site under the silver bars. This is what my instruments tell me anyway.

I have a very good idea of where this treasure is located. At my last testing, it was still there waiting for someone to dig it up and become wealthy. I haven't done it yet because my priorities will not let me at this time. Now that the reader has a pretty good idea where it could be, I say go get it. There is plenty for everyone on this mountain. Just remember this author at Christmas time if you get lucky.

PART FOUR

CHAPTER ELEVEN

THE MULE EARS

A favorite sign of the Spanish was mule ears. The rocks at this site were definitely placed there for a purpose, and the purpose was to mark the way for any future Spaniards who may wander there. Life was uncertain during the Spanish years, but with these signs a knowledgeable person could follow them to any treasure that may lie there. At least in a perfect world that is. In the Caballos Mountains most signs have either been destroyed completely or partially destroyed so that following them is impossible. They were destroyed by greedy treasure hunters who did not want anyone to follow them to their location or by ones who just didn't want to let anyone have a chance of reading them. This is what makes the Mule Ears so unique. They still exist.

Doc Noss, as well as Josie Bell Butler, spoke of using the Mule Ears both as a destination and a landmark. Josie Bell Butler stated in her deathbed testimony that Doc Noss would tie his safety rope off one of the Mule Ears when he lowered himself into the cavern during his forays into the Caballos Mountains.

These Mule Ears are massive and stand beside the Spanish road I wrote about in the Flower of Carmel Mine story.

The ears are about three quarters of a mile above the washed out portion of the Spanish road in Longbottom Canyon.

I believe that this is the location where Doc Noss and Josie Bell entered the mountain. At this writing I have been unable to locate a shallow entrance. My underground radar shows objects below but at this point they remain only tantalizing images on a computer screen. This area is under mineral claim and therefore I have no urgency in pursuing this. Were this area to become open, my interest would increase.

I also have reason to believe that Padre LaRue is buried in this vicinity. On the opposite side of the canyon past the washed out Spanish road there is a Hackberry tree overlooking the wash. Placed in this tree is a stone image of a kneeling priest being held up by the tree's branches on two sides. This stone could not have been placed there by accident or just rolled off the hill and into the tree. Somebody placed it there and I think it may have been the mission Apaches. I consider this a grave marker. The Apaches always used stones to mark their graves so it would be a natural thing to do in this case. I also get a massive gold hit with my long-range metal detector on this site.

This conforms to the Noss/Butler stories, that from under the dead hand of Padre LaRue, maps and descriptions of Victorio Peak emerged. This was also the first verification of the existence of Padre LaRue, who up until this time was just considered a legend. This verification was perhaps the best thing that came from Doc Noss in his quest for treasure in the Caballos Mountains.

CHAPTER TWELVE

THE MONEY PIT

This is a story that really begins with Fred Drolte in the 1960's. It was a time when just about anything one wanted to do on federal land was allowed, or at least overlooked.

It was at Granite Peak and Fred was drilling his fateful hole, that would eventually lead to the abrupt shut down of his operation on the Caballos Mountains. Beside this eight-inch drill hole, Fred had placed a twenty-four inch cased hole that descended 170 feet into the mountain (some say even further). About this time Fred hit the big time (gold bars) and abruptly closed the operation down. This story is about what happened to this claim in the years following Fred's disappearance.

There were three brothers who leased the claims from Fred's widow and it was they who replaced the twenty-four inch casing with thirty-six inch casing that shortened it to one hundred forty feet. From this point a natural cavern opened up below to ancient tunnels. Or so they said. It was these same three brothers who previously filled the thirty-six inch casing up with dirt to prevent people from descending into the mine.

My partner and I gained access to these claims through research and timeliness and took possession of this site. Our job was to remove the dirt from the thirty-six inch casing and it was slow going. Between three of us we gained about four feet a day and it was hard work. Our crew consisted of Ralph Wolak, Lewis Jameson and myself. We were all over fifty and it was beginning to show.

Typically we would lower ourselves down on a harness with a rope tied to the back bumper of the truck then fill buckets until we ran out of steam and needed to be lifted out. It was a precarious and dangerous system and it took a lot of courage to get into the harness and swing out over the hole to be lowered into the darkness. I have always said that a coward dies a thousand deaths but I think I used up half of them on the journey in and out of this hole. The inside of the casing was rough with small protrusions of metal. Even a small scrape would result in a torn shirt or ripped trousers. This project was far and away the most uncomfortable and dangerous thing we attempted on the Caballos Mountains. Did I mention the world-class infections caused by the slightest scratch while in the hole? Lucky for us we had a generous supply of Mexican penicillin.

We had been informed by the two surviving members of Fred Drolte's crew that the gold bars had been hit by the driller between ninety feet and one hundred thirty feet depending upon what day of the week it was. I know they didn't start out this way, but these two would tell a lie if the truth would serve them better. It must have come from years of trying to attract investors into their treasure hunting schemes, or maybe something in the water they drink. Our own equipment showed the precious metal at 123 feet.

We had succeeded in digging the vertical shaft down to eighty-eight feet when it was mutually agreed that something else should be tried. This was much too hard for senior citizens like us.

Then we met the boys from Utah, the answer to our prayers. This hard working crew came on the scene with new ideas and energy at a time when we needed it most. Within two days the shaft was opened but to our great surprise the lower caverns were filled with water. Now what to do? This treasure hunt was getting more and more complicated all the time.

After consulting with one of the brothers who had been in these caverns, we decided to pump the caverns dry to see if there was some blockage causing the water to accumulate here. Here again, the boys from Utah came through again. If I haven't mentioned their names it was Scott Beal, with his son-in-law Ashton and his son Jason, along with Ken Baker doing the driving. This crew arrived in the evening and by the time Ralph Wolak and myself showed up the next morning the cavern had been pumped out and our questions were answered. The lower caverns went nowhere. Within twenty-four hours the water filled back in to its original levels. We would have to try something else.

Next we found a cavern off the vertical shaft at 115 feet that seemed to be heading for the gold bar room. Currently we are exploring this possibility as a way of getting into the gold bars. At this writing we have not succeeded.

I mentioned that this was a dangerous undertaking and it is true. On too many occasions, we have barely avoided one disaster after another. I am happy to report that the only permanent casualty was myself. This project owes me the end of my left index finger, which was pinched off in an open pulley while removing someone from the shaft.

As the reader can see this, is truly becoming a Money Pit as failure after failure continues to drive the costs up.

Remember that treasure hunters are a strange lot. We get up each morning thinking that today could be the day when

Ralph Wolak assists William White into the entrance shaft of the money pit site.

our fortunes are made.   We are the ultimate optimists.

The author William White is photographed in the shaft at 170 feet into the earth.

For more infromation on other publications by
William H. White please write to:

William H. White
P.O. Box 3843
Truth or Consequences
New Mexico 87901
(775) 303-6234

Or visit our website at:

www.williamwhitebooks.com

Or e-mail at:

williamwhitebooks@gmail.com